GW00702058

Essex Buses
In Camera

by
Philip C. Miles

QUOTES LIMITED

MCMXCIV

Published by Quotes Limited
Whittlebury, England

Typeset in Plantin by
Key Composition, Northampton, England

Pictures Lithographed by
South Midlands Lithoplates Limited, Luton, England

Printed by Busiprint Limited
Buckingham, England

Bound by WBC Bookbinders Limited
Bridgend, Glamorgan

© Philip C. Miles 1994

ISBN 0 86023 619 6

Acknowledgements

The author is grateful for all the help he has received from a number of people and would like to thank especially Mr Peter Snell of the Essex Bus Enthusiast Group for information readily given on several Westcliff on Sea vehicles, and Eastern National for allowing access to a well-detailed account of the company.

In a selection of road transport in Essex over the last hundred years or so the task of deciding which photographs to use and which to exclude was difficult. Within a wide area of coverage particular emphasis has been placed on Southend, Colchester, Chelmsford and Clacton.

This book is dedicated with love to my Mother.

Key to Photographers

EBEG	Essex Bus Enthusiast Group
PCMC	Philip C. Miles collection
CLR	C. L. Raynor collection
JF	John Fozard
PJS	P. J. Snell
FC/EBEG	Frank Church/Essex Bus Enthusiast Group
B	Bedford Motors Ltd

FRONT COVER: Silver Queen's Leyland 'G' on services in Clacton. (EBEG)

Until the arrival of mechanical transport in the late 1800s, stage coach was the main way to travel — apart from horseback. Small businesses operated wagonettes, which were simply horse-drawn carts fitted with wooden seats.

Southend on Sea Corporation sought to operate electric trams in September 1899 when a Light Railway Order was granted that authorised their use. Construction commenced in February 1900 and service on 19 July 1901.

In Colchester authorisation was obtained in 1901 to construct an electric tramway of 3ft 6in gauge. Construction started in 1904, the system consisting of three routes from North Station; it opened on 28 July 1904 using a fleet of 18 open-top, four-wheel cars. Withdrawal of the tramway route came with the implementation of the Colchester Corporation Act of 1927. The run-down started on 21 May 1928 and the last tram operated on 8 December 1929. Trolleybuses were never operated in Colchester.

However, Southend Transport was an early user of the trolleybus, operations commencing as early as 1925. The trolleybus system expanded in the 1930s, when existing trams were replaced by them on several routes.

Vehicles were acquired from Teeside Railless Traction Board and Wolverhampton Corporation. In 1934 Southend took delivery of the only Gloster trolleybus ever built. An AEC Q trolleybus was also purchased in 1935.

The National Steam Car Co Ltd was founded in 1909 by Thomas Clarkson, the steam 'bus builder, who started several 'bus services in London at the end of 1909. Clarkson had his works in Chelmsford. The National Steam Car Co Ltd took over the Great Eastern Railway road services in the area in 1913. In 1919 Clarkson withdrew from London

services, expanded the National Company in the Essex area into the 1920s, acquiring many small independents in the process.

Powers to operate motorbuses were obtained by Southend Corporation in 1912 and on 25 June 1914 seven vehicles opened two services. The vehicles were three Tilling-Stevens petrol electric, three Straker Squires and one Edison battery-electric vehicle, all with Brush bodywork, and numbered 1-7 HJ 28-34.

Moore Brothers of Kelvedon had started their business in 1815, and operated the first motor 'bus out of Kelvedon in 1912. Several operators began running soft-top char-a-bancs on excursions as well as on town or rural routes. The char-a-banc was, however, short-lived and soon gave way to the influx of more modern 'buses and coaches in the 1920s.

Colchester Corporation began operating motorbuses in 1928, when both double and single-deck Dennises took over from trams. In 1928 the four main railway companies, Great Western, London Midland Scottish, London North Eastern and Southern Railways, obtained road passenger transport powers and acquired an interest in the National company. National Omnibus (National Steam Car's new name) was to be split into four separate operations: Eastern, Southern, Western and Midland National. The four operators were registered on 28 February 1929. The LMS and LNER lines were located in such a way that it was impossible to define the operating areas of Eastern National and Midland National, so the Eastern National fleetname was used.

In 1931 Thomas Tilling Ltd acquired the remaining capital of the holding company; thus Eastern National came under Tilling control. More independents were taken over, including Borough Motor Services Ltd, in 1933.

In Southend many tram routes were abandoned between 1939-1942, and the last day of operation was 8 April 1942. A total of 68 cars was operated, on a gauge of 3ft 6ins.

Eastern National was nationalised in 1948, when the Tilling Group sold its 'bus interest to the Government and became a member of the British Transport Commission. Part of Eastern National, the Midland section was transferred with 245 vehicles to United Counties on 1 May 1952. Eastern National continued to acquire well-known operators in its remaining area, including Westcliff on Sea Motor Services Ltd, which had been a Tilling company since 1935. Westcliff had itself acquired several operators, including Benfleet & District and City Coach Company Ltd. Expansion of the fleet continued, with many small independents absorbed over the years.

The early 1950s saw the beginning of the end of the trolleybus in Southend. The last day of operation was 28 October 1954, when co-ordination agreement with Eastern National was implemented.

On 1 January 1969, Eastern National became part of the National Bus Company and stayed under NBC control until a management buy-out on 23 December 1986. In April 1990 Eastern National joined the Badgerline Holdings Group; part of it split in 1990 to form a new company called Thamesway Ltd.

1994 is the 90th anniversary of the first electric tram to be operated in Colchester. Both Southend and Colchester Corporation Transport are now owned by British Bus. Since de-regulation in the late 1980s, several small independents are once again emerging and taking on the larger companies, adding even more interest to Essex 'buses.

ABOVE: *Tramway operation commenced in Southend on Sea on 19 July 1901. Fourteen Brush cars were purchased. Numbers 1-10 were Brill 21E four-wheel 38-seat open-top cars. Car number 8 is seen on the newly opened Beach extension. (CLR) OPPOSITE: An early form of psv was the steam 'bus. Clarkson began building these at Chelmsford as early as 1903. F233 is the original Clarkson steam 'bus. (EBEG)*

Southend Corporation Tramways purchased three Brush 58-seat open-top cars in 1902 with Brush bogies. In 1906 they were rebuilt with Brush 22E bogies. They had canopies fitted and the seating increased to 72 in 1912. In 1927 they were converted to enclosed top. Car number 16 is seen in this form. (EBEG)

Silver Queen operated NO 6623, an early open-top, open-staircased Leyland 'G', on services in the Clacton area. Silver Queen Motor Omnibus Co Ltd was an early acquisition for the newly-formed Eastern National Company in September 1931. (EBEG)

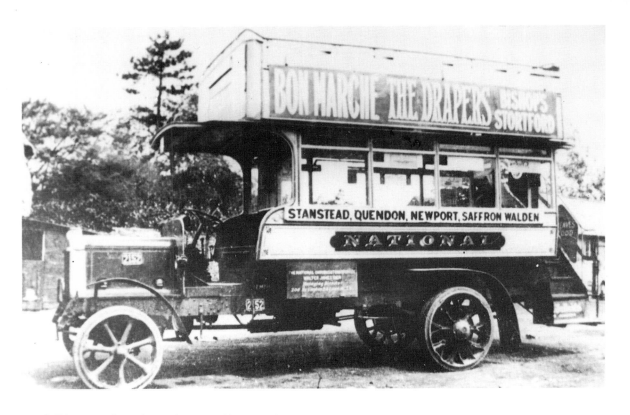

Solid tyres and wooden spokes are evident on this AEC 'Y' in the National Omnibus & Transport fleet; it was numbered 2152. The 'Y' was one of the most popular chassis for double-deck 'buses in the early 1920s. (EBEG)

Seven Brush trams were added to the Southend fleet in 1912. These were 30-36, fifty-eight-seat open-top cars and 37-39, 70-seat open-top cars. One of the latter is number 37, rebuilt in 1925 with an English Electric enclosed covered top. (EBEG)

All eyes turn to the photographer in this fully-laden Daimler char-a-banc (HJ4858), once in the fleet of Westcliff Motor Company. Note the rolled down canvas roof at the back of the vehicle. (EBEG)

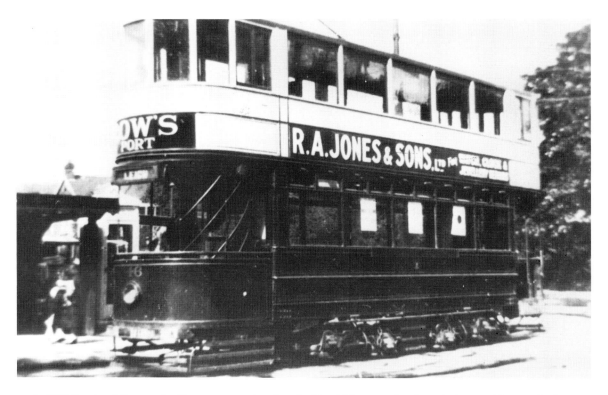

In 1921 Southend Corporation Tramways purchased twelve Brush 70-seat enclosed top-deck cars with open platform and fitted with Peckham P23 bogies. One of the batch, number 46, is seen here on the Leigh service. This car was not withdrawn until 1942. (EBEG)

Borough Motor Services operated this early Gilford saloon. (EBEG)

The char-a-banc in its heyday: this Daimler belonged to Hicks Bros. Char-a-banc is derived from the French for 'carriage with seats'. (EBEG)

The driver of this Westcliff on Sea Motors char-a-banc poses proudly with his vehicle, photographed outside the depôt.
(EBEG)

The char-a-banc was short-lived, and replaced in the mid 1920s by coaches more appropriately designed for the modern passenger. This all-weather luxury motor-coach is a Leyland TS2, number 2861 (UU 1267) in the National Omnibus & Transport fleet. (EBEG)

Photographed on the Kurstall Beach and Thorpe Bay route is number 31, a 1910 Brush 52-seat open-top car in the Southend Corporation Tramways fleet. (EBEG)

Southend Corporation Transport number 116 (JN 2086) was an AEC demonstrator built in 1930, originally registered HX 1460. It is an AEC 663T with an EEC body; when new it had a full front. Sold to Southend in 1932, it was originally fitted with dual staircase and dual doors. The front staircase and entrance were later removed and it was converted to full front. (EBEG)

In 1932, Eastern National took delivery of this impressive three-axled AEC Renown with Short L66R body. It became Eastern National 3332 (MJ 406). The larger (66) seating capacity should be compared with standard capacity of the time at some 48 seats. (EBEG)

A view of the impressive 'bus station at Chelmsford c1935; visible are Thornycrofts, AEC and Leyland double-deck 'buses. (EBEG)

Southend Corporation Transport number 114 (JN 2114) was a 1932 AEC 661T trolleybus with an EEC L46R body and fitted with a dummy radiator; this was removed in 1948. Number 114 saw twenty-one years of service with Southend Corporation until the closure of the system in 1954. (EBEG)

HX 2980 was an AEC demonstrator new in 1932, later acquired by Westcliff on Sea Motors, who converted it to an open-top vehicle. It is an AEC Regent I with an ECW 56 seat body. (PCMC)

In 1946, Southend Corporation Transport acquired secondhand 'buses from several operators, including Nottingham City Transport, Mansfield District Traction and Leeds City Transport. From Leeds came number 248 (UG 1030), a 1932 AEC Regent with a Roe H56R body. It was formerly Leeds City Transport number 43. (EBEG)

Eastern National 3068 (EV 1947) is a Thornycroft XC and is fitted with a Strachan L48R body. (EBEG)

Eastern National number 3656 (EHD 934) entered service in 1937 and is a Leyland Titan TD4. It was photographed in its original pre-war condition. (EBEG)

In 1934, Southend Corporation acquired three Brush 72-seat cars, with Brush swing-wing bogies, from Accrington Corporation. Number 66 was new in 1915 and 67/68 new in 1920. They were numbered 39/40/41 in the Accrington fleet. Car 66 shows the five-bay construction. (CLR)

This Dennis Lance with BHD bodywork was acquired by Westcliff on Sea Motors from Brighton Hove & District. NJ5976 was part of a batch of six bought mainly for contract work; however, NJ 5976 was converted to open-top and fitted with an AEC radiator. (EBEG)

Southend Corporation Transport purchased seven AEC Regents with Weymann L27/26R bodies in 1938. Number 211 (AHJ 831), the first of the batch, was photographed on its way to Leigh Church on service 25B. (EBEG)

The City Coach Company bought this four-wheel-steering Leyland Gnu, fitted with a Duple 39-seat coach body, in 1939. It was a regular coach on the London to Southend service. The Gnu was an attempt to increase the seating capacity of coaches. This one was numbered C6 (HVW 214) in the City Coach fleet. (EBEG)

Westcliff on Sea Motors JN 8566 was a Bristol J05G with an ECOC B35R body. (PCMC)

This Bristol K5G with a Bristol H56R bodywork was purchased by Colchester Corporation Transport in 1942, in whose fleet it became number 35 (JPU 581). Although built to war-time utility standards it had upholstered seats fitted. (EBEG)

The normal control version of the AEC Regal was the Ranger; Westcliff on Sea Motors' AHJ 843 had a Duple 24-seat body. (PCMC)

Colchester Corporation Transport bought nothing but AECs in the 1930s, including number 31 (GVW 947), a 1939 Regent with a Massey 52-seat rear-entrance body. (EBEG)

The ECW body carried by the Bristol K was attractive, well-designed and well-proportioned, as can be seen on Eastern National number 1250 (ENO 932) — a design that never seemed to date. (JF)

The Bristol JO5G was introduced in 1931, powered by a Gardner 5-cylinder oil unit. Westcliff on Sea Motors number 230 (JN 6889) carries a rear-entrance 35-seat ECOC body. (PCMC)

Five Bristol K6As were purchased by Colchester Corporation Transport in 1945, two with Duple H56R bodies and three with Park Royal H56R bodies. Number 46 (KEV 331) carries a Duple body. They were built to utility standards. (EBEG)

Six Daimler CVD6s with Massey L27/26R bodies were added to the Southend Corporation Transport fleet in 1949.
Number 251 (DHJ 427) was the first of the batch and is seen on route 5A. The trolleybus wires are overhead.
(EBEG)

In 1951, only two vehicles were bought by Colchester Corporation Transport — two Crossley DD42/7s with Crossley 56-seat rear-entrance bodies. Number 7 (SVW 451) is seen alongside 'bus number 28 (9671 VX), a 1960 Leyland Titan PD2/31 with Massey H61R bodywork. (FC/EBEG)

This Guy Arab had a chequered history; it was originally with Birch Bros of Royal Mail Yard in north London; it was later purchased by Moore Bros of Kelvedon. Eastern National purchased Moore Brothers in 1963 and it was numbered 1027 (GYL 982) by Eastern National. It carries a Strachan L56R body. (JF)

Colchester Corporation Transport purchased four AEC Regents in 1947, with Massey 56-seat rear-entrance bodies. One of this batch is number 52 (KPU 516), which was not withdrawn until 1966. (EBEG)

Eastern National Omnibus Company number 294 (MPU 26) is a Bristol L, with an attractive ECW body. It is seen with more cream than was usual on stage service 'buses and was used as a dual-purpose vehicle. (FC)

City Coach Company number C7 (LPU 690) is a 1948 Commer Q4 and fitted with a Heaver B33F body. It later passed to Eastern National as their 157, with the business of Westcliff on Sea Motors. (EBEG)

A number of utility 'buses were purchased by Southend Corporation Transport during the war years. One such vehicle was number 224 (BHJ 773), a 1944 Daimler CWA6 with Brush utility 55-seat rear-entrance body. Utility bodies were pretty basic with straight, uncurved panels which saved many hours of panel beating. (EBEG)

A number of secondhand trolleybuses were acquired by Southend Corporation Transport, including in 1950 number 147 (BDA 367), an ex-Wolverhampton Corporation Sunbeam MF2 with a Park Royal 54-seat rear-entrance body. It was new in 1937 and was numbered 267 in the Wolverhampton fleet. (EBEG)

In 1948, Colchester Corporation Transport bought number 55 (KPU 519), a Crossley DD42/3T, fitted with a Massey H30/26R body. Number 55 operated for two weeks on a trial basis with a torque converter but after the trials a normal gearbox was fitted. (EBEG)

Southend Corporation Transport purchased one Daimler CWG5 and six CWA6s from Eastern National Omnibus Co Ltd in 1955. Number 246 (JVW 561) is a CWA6 with a Duple 56-seat rear-entrance body. New in 1944 to the Benfleet and District Motor Transport Company, it passed to Westcliff on Sea Motors in 1951 and to Eastern National in 1955. (EBEG)

Southend 246 (JVW 561) was converted to open-top in 1957 by Southend Corporation. It remained in operation in this guise until withdrawn in 1970. (EBEG)

Two Bristol L6Bs with Eastern Coachworks bodywork, EHJ 27 and EHJ 28 of 1950, in the fleet of Westcliff on Sea Motors, are here on a full day tour. (PCMC)

Colchester Corporation Transport number 3 (OHK 431) is a Daimler CVD6 with a Roberts H56R body. It was new in 1949 and was not withdrawn until 1968. (EBEG)

Westcliff on Sea Motors operated several AEC Regals with attractive half-cab and front-entrance Duple bodies. One such vehicle on the London service is number 149 (BJN 117). They were delivered in 1939 but not used till after the war. (PCMC)

Westcliff on Sea Motors operated a number of Bedford OBs. One such vehicle is number 214 (DJN 553), which carries an attractive Duple C29F body. 214 was part of the batch DJN 548/51-3. (PCMC)

Carrying the Westcliff on Sea fleet name and fleet number 362 (EJN 638) is this 1952 Bristol LS6G with ECW C39F bodywork. It is seen at London Victoria station. Certain coaches retained the Westcliff on Sea fleet name for about two years after the take-over by Eastern National (PCMC)

Colchester Corporation Transport purchased three AEC Regent MkIIIs in 1953 and had them fitted with Massey 56-seat rear-entrance bodywork. Number 12 (WPU 734) was the last of the batch. (PCMC)

Massey bodywork was chosen by Southend Corporation Transport for five Leyland Titan PD2/20s in 1954. These were of low height design and fitted with the 'tin front'. Number 277 (HJN 837) was a 56-seater rear-entrance vehicle and awaits more passengers before setting off on the 25A service. (PCMC)

Here in Jubilee livery is Colchester Corporation Transport number 9 (TVX 497), a 1952 Crossley DD42/7 fitted with a Crossley H56R body. (EBEG)

Open-top 'buses are a popular sight in Essex, operated by Southend Transport, Eastern National and in the past by the now defunct Westcliff on Sea Motors. Eastern National 2382 (WNO 478) is a 1953 Bristol KSW5G with an ECW 033/28R body, converted to open-top in 1966. (EBEG)

A number of BTC operators purchased the Bristol SC4LK with ECW 35-seat front-entrance bodies, for use mainly on rural routes. Eastern National was one south-east operator to purchase the SC4LK, illustrated here by number 440 (610 JPU). (FC/EBEG)

The Southend trolleybus system closed on 28 October 1954 and trolleybus number 128 (BHJ 198), a 1939 AEC 661T with a Strachan H36/26R body, is seen decorated as the last vehicle to be operated. (EBEG)

This Bristol LS5G was delivered new to Westcliff on Sea Motors and then had an ECW 39-seat front entrance and rear exit. The rear exit was later removed and it became a 41-seater. Number 378 (FJN 162) is here in its original condition. (PCMC)

In 1954, Eastern National took delivery of a new type of double-deck 'bus, the Bristol Lodekka with ECW bodywork. Number 2444 (501 EEV) shows the deep radiator grille common on early Bristol Lodekka LDs. The Lodekka was to become Eastern National's standard 'bus for many years to come. (PCMC)

In 1958, Southend Transport took delivery of numbers 311-316 (PHJ 950-5), Leyland Titan PD3/6s with attractive Massey L35/33R bodies. Of this batch 311-4 were rebuilt during the winter of 1970/1 to open-top for the sea-front service. Number 314 is in the new open-top livery. (EBEG)

Four AEC Regent MkVs, with attractive Massey H33/28R bodies, were purchased by Colchester Corporation Transport in 1956 and numbered 13-16 (679-682 HEV). Number 15 as delivered was renumbered several times while with Colchester, becoming number 55 in 1973 and then number 5 in 1975, the year it was withdrawn. (EBEG)

Ordered by City Coach Company, but delivered to Westcliff on Sea Motors after the former's takeover, number 133 (FJN 212) was a Leyland Leopard PSU1, fitted with a Burlingham 39-seat central entrance body. (PCMC)

Eastern National purchased large numbers of Bristol Lodekkas with standard ECW bodies from 1956 until the mid-1960s. Number 2506 (1851 F) is an LD model and carries the smaller and much more attractive front grille.
(PJS)

Southend Corporation Transport took delivery of number 201 (SJN 635), an Albion MR11L with a Weymann 45-seat front-entrance body, in 1959. (PCMC)

Southend Corporation Transport purchased four AEC Bridgemasters, numbers 319-322 with Park Royal H45/31R bodies, in 1960. This is the first of the batch, number 319 (WHJ 430). Southend had bought two Bridgemasters numbers 317-318 in 1959 but the four in 1960 were the last. (PCMC)

The 1961 delivery for Southend Corporation Transport consisted of only two vehicles, numbers 206-207 (2717-8 HJ), Leyland Leopard L1s fitted with Weymann 43-seat dual-door bodywork. Number 207 is on service 9B. (PCMC)

Carrying the Westcliff on Sea name on the bodywork and the Eastern National name in the destination box is number 457 (7016 HK), a Bristol MW with an Eastern Coach Works C39F body. (PCMC)

Southend Corporation purchased ten Leyland (Albion) Lowlander LR7s in 1963 with Alexander H41/29F bodies. One of the batch, number 325 (7089 HJ), shows the uneasy style of bodywork fitted to this type of vehicle. The Lowlanders were fitted for one-person operation between 1969 and 1970. Front-engined vehicles were never suited to this type of operation, due to the driver having to turn in his/her seat at an angle to collect the fares. (PCMC)

This Leyland Worldmaster RT3/1 with a Weymann/GCT, B44F body was new to Glasgow Corporation Transport in 1956 as their LS8. It was purchased by Southend Corporation Transport in 1966 and became number 212 (FYS 679) in the Southend fleet. (EBEG)

Southend Corporation Transport number 334 (CJN 434C) was a 1965 Leyland Titan PD3/6 with Massey H38/32R body. Here, 334 is passing Eastern National number 1346 (206 YVX), a Bristol MW5G with an ECW B45F body. (EBEG)

In 1971, Colchester Corporation Transport bought six AEC Reliances with Weymann B45F bodies from SELNEC. Numbered 1-6 (TRJ 109/102-6) by Colchester, these vehicles were new in 1962 to Salford City Transport, in whose fleet they were numbered 102-6/9; when SELNEC PTE was formed in 1969 they became numbers 65-9/71 in the PTE fleet. Number 6 (TRJ 106) was fitted for one-man operation before entering service with Colchester. (EBEG)

The first Daimler Fleetlines for Southend Transport were not purchased until 1971, when twenty-six CRL6/33s with Northern Counties 80-seat dual-doorway bodywork entered service. Number 366 (WJN 366) is passing the Tarpot public house on limited-stop service 400. (PJS)

A number of municipals purchased the Bristol RE. Colchester Corporation Transport bought five RELL6Ls with attractive ECW 53-seat front-entrance bodies in 1972. First of the batch was number 24 (SWC 24K), here on service 5. (EBEG)

To celebrate the Queen's Silver Jubilee in 1977, several operators painted their 'buses in a special livery. Colchester Corporation Transport number 55 (JHK 495N), a 1975 Leyland Atlantean AN68/1R with an ECW H43/31F body, is here in Silver Jubilee livery. (PJS)

Ten Leyland Fleetline FE33ALRs with Northern Counties H49/31D bodies, numbered 221-230 (XTE 221-30V), were purchased by Southend Transport in 1979. One of the batch is number 228 (XTE 228V), seen here without fleet name or crest. (PCMC)

Westcliff on Sea Motors operated this AEC Regal with its attractive Duple body; BJN 117 was new in 1939. (PCMC)

A Bedford selection: On the left is Eastern National number 1204 (BNO 690T), a 53-seat Duple Dominant Express II on Bedford YMT, new in 1978. Centre is Bedford's first coach, a WHB with Waveney 14-seat bodywork; the WHB was introduced in 1931. On the right is a Plaxton Supreme 53-seater in the fleet of Premier Albanian. (B)

Index to Illustrations